CW01649215

MAD ABOUT LIVERPOOL

FACTS, TRIVIA AND QUIZZES FOR DIE-HARD FANS

summersdale

MAD ABOUT LIVERPOOL

Copyright © Octopus Publishing Group Limited, 2025

Text by Peter Salmon

All rights reserved.

No part of this book may be reproduced by any means, nor transmitted, nor translated into a machine language, without the written permission of the publishers.

Condition of Sale
This book is sold subject to the condition that it shall not, by way of trade or otherwise, be lent, resold, hired out or otherwise circulated in any form of binding or cover other than that in which it is published and without a similar condition including this condition being imposed on the subsequent purchaser.

An Hachette UK Company
www.hachette.co.uk

Summersdale Publishers
Part of Octopus Publishing Group Limited
Carmelite House
50 Victoria Embankment
LONDON
EC4Y 0DZ
UK

www.summersdale.com

ISBN: 978-1-83799-868-5

Substantial discounts on bulk quantities of Summersdale books are available to corporations, professional associations and other organizations. For details contact general enquiries: telephone: +44 (0) 1243 771107 or email: enquiries@summersdale.com.

This book is unofficial and is not endorsed by or in any other way connected with Liverpool. Every effort has been made to ensure that all information is correct. Should there be any errors, we apologize and shall be pleased to make the appropriate amendments in any future editions.

To..

From..

INTRODUCTION

Lots of clubs vie for the title of the greatest football team in England, but there can only ever be one real answer – the mighty Liverpool! With (at the time of writing) 19 league titles, eight FA Cups, a record ten League Cups and 16 FA Community Shields in domestic competitions, along with six European Cups, three UEFA Cups, four UEFA Super Cups – all English records – and one FIFA Club World Cup internationally, the trophy cabinet is bursting.

From Bill Shankly's incredible teams of the 1960s to the trophy-winning machines of the 1970s and 80s, through to the new champions of the Jürgen Klopp era, Liverpool has terrorized opponents for many years.

Players like Steven Gerrard, Kevin Keegan, Michael Owen, Ian Rush, Mohamed (Mo) Salah and Kenny Dalglish have been the envy of other supporters. With the best players and fans, every Liverpool supporter knows that "You'll Never Walk Alone".

”

We are Liverpool Football Club and the expectations are so high.

STEVEN GERRARD

DID YOU KNOW...

Liverpool was founded in 1892, making them one of England's oldest clubs. They joined the Football League a year later, and won their first championship in 1900–01. They have always played at the same home ground, Anfield – one of the most iconic football grounds in the world!

TRIVIA

Liverpool's nineteenth league title in 2019–20 was their first since which year?

a) 1987–88

b) 1989–90

c) 1990–91

> We always said we had the best two teams on Merseyside – Liverpool and Liverpool reserves.

BILL SHANKLY

DID YOU KNOW...

In their debut year, before joining the Football League, Liverpool played in the Lancashire League – and came out champions! They finished ahead of Blackpool on goal difference, despite losing to them twice in the season. Their first captain, Andrew Hannah, had previously captained arch-rival Everton!

TRIVIA

Steven Gerrard holds the record for the most games as Liverpool captain, with 471. Whose record did be break?

a) Emlyn Hughes

b) Ron Yeats

c) Alan Hansen

”

I am still a Liverpool fan and will be forever, absolutely.

XABI ALONSO

DID YOU KNOW...

There are lots of reasons for the rivalry between Liverpool and Everton, but one is that when they shared Anfield as a home ground, from 1884–92, the Liverpool chairman was a brewer, while several people on the board at Everton were Temperance Society members – aiming to ban drinking!

TRIVIA

Which Liverpool player became the first from the club to win the Golden Boot since Michael Owen back in the 1990s?

a) Mohamed Salah

b) Luis Suárez

c) Sadio Mané

Liverpool are magic.
Everton are tragic.

EMLYN HUGHES

DID YOU KNOW...

When legendary manager Bill Shankly took over the club in 1959, it had been in the Second Division for five years. He won them promotion by winning the title in 1961–62, and two years later they won the First Division, the first of three under Shankly (plus two FA Cups).

TRIVIA

In the Premier League era, which Liverpool player has the most red cards?

a) Steven Gerrard

b) Jamie Carragher

c) Javier Mascherano

”

If Shankly was the Anfield foreman, Paisley was the brickie, ready to build an empire with his own hands.

TOMMY SMITH

DID YOU KNOW...

When Sami Hyypiä took over as captain of Liverpool in 2002, he became the club's first overseas skipper. The Finnish international had supported Liverpool as a boy, and played 464 games for the club in ten seasons for the Reds, including the 2004–05 Champions League triumph.

TRIVIA

Who scored twice in Liverpool's 2001 FA Cup triumph against Arsenal, after the Reds were down 1-0 with seven minutes to play?

a) Michael Owen

b) Emile Heskey

c) Robbie Fowler

”

Football is the most important of the least important things.

JÜRGEN KLOPP

DID YOU KNOW...

The famous grandstand at Anfield, called the Kop, is named for its resemblance to a mountain called Spion Kop, near Ladysmith in South Africa, site of a famous battle in the Boer War! The stand holds 13,000 fans, known as Kopites, down from 25,000 when it was standing room.

TRIVIA

In the 2005 Champions League win against AC Milan, Liverpool goalkeeper Jerzy Dudek pulled off what he called "the save of my life" in the hundred-and-seventeenth minute. Whose shot did he save?

a) Hernán Crespo

b) Kaká

c) Andriy Shevchenko

> I couldn't settle in Italy – it was like living in a foreign country.

IAN RUSH

DID YOU KNOW...

No English club had provided more England captains than Liverpool, with 12 Reds taking the armband. The player with the most games as captain is Steven Gerrard with 38, ahead of Kevin Keegan on 31. The first man to do so was Ephraim Longworth in 1921, only his second England game.

TRIVIA

Michael Owen is the only Liverpool player to have won the Ballon d'Or, in 2001. But Liverpool legend Kevin Keegan won it twice, playing for which German club?

a) Bayern Munich

b) Hamburger HSV

c) Borussia Mönchengladbach

”

To work hard and have our supporters behind us and believing until the end, you run a little bit more.

RAFAEL BENÍTEZ

DID YOU KNOW...

Liverpool achieved its first League and FA Cup Double in 1985–86, Kenny Dalglish's first year as player-manager. They beat arch-rivals Everton in the Cup Final 3–1, who they also pushed down into second in the League by winning the final game 1–0 against Chelsea. Dalglish scored the goal!

TRIVIA

Liverpool hold the record for the earliest title win in 2019–20. How many games were still to be played?

a) 5

b) 6

c) 7

> I love tackling, it's better than sex!

PAUL INCE

DID YOU KNOW...

In September 2019, Harvey Elliott became the youngest player to ever start a match for Liverpool, aged 16 years, 5 months, 21 days. But he's not the youngest to play for the Reds – Jerome Sinclair came off the bench against West Bromwich Albion in 2012 at 16 years, 6 days.

TRIVIA

Liverpool went a club-record 44 games without a defeat in the Premier League from 12 January 2019 to 24 February 2020 on their way to the title, before losing to what eventually relegated team 3–0?

a) Bournemouth

b) Norwich City

c) Watford

”

These players are my true heroes.

GERARD HOULLIER

DID YOU KNOW...

Striker Ian Rush holds the record for the most goals for Liverpool, scoring 346 in 660 games, way ahead of Roger Hunt's 285. A boyhood Everton fan, Rush was recruited from Chester in 1980. His 41 goals in the FA Cup are a record, five of them in the final.

TRIVIA

Liverpool played in Europe for the first time in 1964 against an Icelandic team they beat 0–5 and 6–1, and have never played since. Who were they?

a) Fimleikafélag Hafnarfjarðar

b) Íþróttabandalag Vestmannaeyja

c) Knattspyrnufélag Reykjavíkur

”

There is no one anywhere in the world at any stage who is any bigger or any better than this football club.

KENNY DALGLISH

DID YOU KNOW...

Liverpool's most successful manager is Bob Paisley (1974-83) with six Football League titles, six Charity Shields, three Football League Cups, three European Cups, one UEFA Super Cup and one UEFA Cup in his nine-year reign as manager. He also won Manager of the Year a record six times!

TRIVIA

Liverpool's greatest away win in a League game came in 2020, when they won 7-0. Which team did they defeat?

a) Crystal Palace

b) Sheffield Wednesday

c) Burnley

> My idea was to build Liverpool up, and up, and up. Eventually, everyone would have to submit, and give in.

BILL SHANKLY

DID YOU KNOW...

It is known as the "Miracle in Istanbul". Down 3–0 at half time against AC Milan, Liverpool scored three goals in six minutes. The game went to extra time and then to penalties, and the Reds won. Vladimír Šmicer will be remembered forever for his incredible long-range goal.

TRIVIA

When Spain won the World Cup in 2010, the squad had two Liverpool players. One was Fernando Torres. Who was the other?

a) Xabi Alonso

b) Pepe Reina

c) Albert Riera

I think every player listens out for his name being sung and it's something I really enjoy.

STEVEN GERRARD

DID YOU KNOW...

Between 1975 and 1990, Liverpool won the League an astonishing ten times. In 1975–76 they won eight of their last nine matches to pip QPR by a point. Few would have imagined it was the start of such a dominant era – in fact, the most dominant in English football.

TRIVIA

When Liverpool won their first FA Cup in 1964–65, beating Leeds 2–1, Roger Hunt scored one of their goals. Who scored the other?

a) Ian Callaghan

b) Ian St John

c) Peter Thompson

I've grown up with Kenny Dalglish; now, to be signed by him is a massive honour.

CRAIG BELLAMY

DID YOU KNOW...

The Hillsborough Disaster is one of the greatest tragedies in the history of football. Liverpool were playing Nottingham Forest in the 1989 FA Cup semi-final when standing-room pens for Liverpool supporters became overcrowded. Ninety-seven fans were crushed to death and 766 suffered injuries.

TRIVIA

Which Liverpool player has scored the most goals in Merseyside derbies?

a) Steve Gerrard

b) Peter Beardsley

c) Ian Rush

”

Derby games are about more than points in the league, or cup victories, they are about bragging rights.

DAVID JAMES

DID YOU KNOW…

After failing to win a hat-trick of first division titles in 1977-78 and again in 1980-81, Liverpool finally managed three in a row 1981-82, 1982-83 and 1983-84, only the third side in history to do so after Huddersfield and Arsenal.

TRIVIA

Liverpool first won the European Cup (later the Champions League) in 1977. Which defender scored a penalty for the third goal?

a) Joey Jones

b) Emlyn Hughes

c) Phil Neal

”

Everyone that plays for Liverpool always stays in the Liverpool family.

VIRGIL VAN DIJK

DID YOU KNOW...

Ian Callaghan holds the record for the most games for Liverpool – 857. A midfielder, who began at Second Division Liverpool in 1960, he played until 1978, winning the title five times, along with two FA Cups, plus two UEFA Cups and the European Cup. He was only ever booked once!

TRIVIA

Liverpool's anthem, "You'll Never Walk Alone", was a hit for Gerry and the Pacemakers in 1963. But which 1945 Rodgers and Hammerstein musical is it taken from?

a) South Pacific

b) Oklahoma!

c) Carousel

"When I score, I don't celebrate because it's my job. When a postman delivers letters, does he celebrate?"

MARIO BALOTELLI

DID YOU KNOW...

Goalkeeper Ray Clemence is usually regarded as the finest player to keep goal at Liverpool. He played 665 games for the club, winning three European Cups, five League titles, two UEFA Cups, a European Super Cup, an FA Cup and a League Cup. He kept 323 clean sheets!

?

TRIVIA

Brilliant winger and midfielder John Barnes played 407 games for Liverpool scored 108 goals after coming to England age 12. He also played over 200 games for which club?

a) Newcastle United

b) Watford

c) Aston Villa

"I am not a dreamer. I am a football romantic.

JÜRGEN KLOPP

DID YOU KNOW...

Three players have scored for both Liverpool and Everton in a Merseyside derby. Two are Peter Beardsley and David Johnson, who played for both teams. The other is Sandy Brown, who scored for Liverpool (an own goal) in 1969, to add to his Everton goal in 1966!

TRIVIA

Whose 359-game career at Liverpool finished with his third European Cup win in 1984, in which he scored during the penalty shootout?

a) Craig Johnston

b) Graeme Souness

c) Alan Kennedy

”

It’s not about the long ball or the short ball, it’s about the right ball.

BOB PAISLEY

DID YOU KNOW...

The first ever overseas-born Liverpool player was from the United States. Hugh Lester's English parents had settled there, but soon returned. Lester only played twice for Liverpool, debuting on 8 April 1912 in a 2–0 victory over Bradford City. He then joined Oldham – playing once!

TRIVIA

In 2018–19, Sadio Mané and Mo Salah became the first teammates to share the Golden Boot with 22 goals. Which opposition player also scored 22?

a) Pierre-Emerick Aubameyang

b) Jamie Vardy

c) Harry Kane

”

If Everton were playing at the bottom of my garden, I’d shut the curtains.

BILL SHANKLY

DID YOU KNOW...

One goal-scoring record not held by Ian Rush is most hat-tricks. Between 1926 and 1935, Gordon Hodgson scored 233 times in 358 games, including 17 hat-tricks – Rush only scored 16! Hodgson also played 56 first-class cricket matches for Lancashire, winning two county championships.

TRIVIA

Who was the first Liverpool manager to win the LMA Manager of the Year award?

a) Brendan Rogers

b) Jürgen Klopp

c) Rafael Benítez

”

Sometimes I feel I’m hardly wanted… if I get two or three saves to make I’ve had a busy day.

RAY CLEMENCE

DID YOU KNOW...

Liverpool have won the Charity Shield 16 times, including a three-peat in 1988, 1989 and 1990. In the 1988 win, John Aldridge scored both goals, the first two of 34 for the year, making him Liverpool's top scorer that season. He played 104 times for Liverpool, scoring 63 goals.

TRIVIA

What astonishing feat did Ephraim Longworth, who played from 1910–28, achieve in his 370 appearances for Liverpool?

a) He never received a yellow card

b) He was never dropped

c) He never scored a goal

> Theres no noise like the Anfield noise.
>
> IAN ST JOHN

DID YOU KNOW...

When Pepe Reina kept goal for Liverpool in the 2007 Champions League Final against Milan, he was matching the feat achieved by his father, Miguel, in 1974 for Atlético Madrid. Unfortunately, he also matched the result – both Reinas were on the losing side.

TRIVIA

Which overseas-born player has played the most times for Liverpool?

a) John Arne Riise

b) Bruce Grobbelaar

c) Jan Mølby

> The most important relationship at a football club is not between the manager and the chairman, but players and fans.

JOHN TOSHACK

DID YOU KNOW...

Liverpool first won the UEFA Super Cup in 1977, beating Hamburger SV. The away game was a 1-1 draw, but at home they trounced the German team 6-0 with Terry McDermott scoring a hat-trick. One disappointed Hamburger player was Kevin Keegan, back at Anfield for the first time.

TRIVIA

Ned Doig is Liverpool's oldest player ever, playing his last game in April 1908, at the age of 41 years and 165 days. Which modern player came closest to breaking that record?

a) Gary McAllister

b) Kolo Touré

c) James Milner

”

Liverpool said I was really important. That made me very proud and at that point I focussed my thoughts on Liverpool.

DIRK KUYT

DID YOU KNOW...

Liverpool has had more success in Europe than any other English side. The team's first victory was in the 1972–73 UEFA Cup, beating Borussia Mönchengladbach. They won the home leg 3–0, but Borussia had two goals at half time in the away. Liverpool clung on to take the title.

TRIVIA

In which legendary room did Bill Shankly discuss tactics?

a) The Locker Room

b) The Boot Room

c) The Board Room

”

Anybody who plays for me should be a bad loser.

GRAEME SOUNESS

DID YOU KNOW...

Liverpool's first Treble came in 1983–84, winning the League, League Cup and European Cup under first-year manager Joe Fagan. Four players played 67 games that year – Alan Hansen, Alan Kennedy, Sammy Lee and Bruce Grobbelaar. It is regarded as one of the greatest teams in world football history.

TRIVIA

Which Liverpool player finished third in the 2008 Ballon d'Or, behind Christiano Ronaldo and Lionel Messi?

a) Steven Gerrard

b) Fernando Torres

c) Xabi Alonso

”

We don’t have any splits here. The players’ country is Liverpool Football Club and their language is football.

GÉRARD HOULLIER

DID YOU KNOW...

Alan Hansen was the first outfield player to win trophies in three different decades, with eight championships, two FA Cups, three League Cups, and three European Cups between 1977 and 1990. He played 620 games, 195 of them as captain, making the PFA team of the year six times.

TRIVIA

Which Belgian club did Liverpool defeat 1-0 in the 1978 European Cup final to secure back-to-back victories?

a) Club Brugge

b) Anderlecht

c) Standard de Liège

”

It’s like a toaster, the ref’s shirt pocket. Every time there’s a tackle, up pops a yellow card.

KEVIN KEEGAN

DID YOU KNOW...

When Egyptian star Mo Salah scored the opener against Lille in the Champions League in January 2025, it was his fiftieth goal in Europe, a record for a player from the Premier League. Second is Arsenal's Thierry Henry, who scored 42. It took Salah just 82 games!

TRIVIA

What was the nickname of inspirational 1970s captain, Emlyn Hughes?

a) Mad Dog

b) Berserk Warrior

c) Crazy Horse

”

If you’re not sure what to do with the ball, just pop it in the net and we’ll discuss your options afterwards.

BILL SHANKLY

DID YOU KNOW...

The fastest ever goal scored by Liverpool took 14 seconds, courtesy of Paul Walsh against West Ham (his first ever goal) in 1984. He later played in Tottenham's 1991 FA Cup win, but was kicked out of the club for punching a goalkeeping coach – Liverpool legend Ray Clemence!

TRIVIA

Liverpool grabbed Jürgen Klopp from Borussia Dortmund in 2015, but he had started his managerial career with which German club, then in the Second Division?

a) Schalke

b) Karlsruher

c) Mainz

> Let's get this clear: I want Manchester United to lose every time they play. I'm pleased when they lose.

JAMIE CARRAGHER

DID YOU KNOW...

The 2021–22 PFA Team of the Year included six Reds, equalling a record from 1982–83. Alisson Becker, Trent Alexander-Arnold, Virgil van Dijk, Thiago Alcântara, Mo Salah and Sadio Mané were picked. The 1982–83 group was Mark Lawrenson, Alan Hansen, Graeme Souness, Sammy Lee, Ian Rush and Kenny Dalglish.

TRIVIA

Who scored the fastest hat-trick in Liverpool history, coming in at four minutes and 33 seconds?

a) Michael Owen

b) Peter Crouch

c) Robbie Fowler

> We play with 11 men, other teams play with 10 men and a goalkeeper.

BRENDAN RODGERS

DID YOU KNOW...

Liverpool's first ever back-to-back title wins came in 1921–22 and 1922–23, both by a comfortable six points. Their star player was Harry "Smiler" Chambers with 21 and 25 goals. In total he scored 151 goals in 339 appearances for Liverpool. He later played for West Brom – as centre-back!

TRIVIA

There were three Liverpool members of England's victorious World Cup-winning squad in 1966, Roger Hunt, Ian Callaghan and who?

a) Peter Thomson

b) Gerry Byrne

c) Gordon Milne

”

The best word I can say to describe this is: Boom!

JÜRGEN KLOPP

DID YOU KNOW...

The Merseyside derby may be ancient, but it still has a bite. In the Premier League era, it holds the record for the most red cards: 23 and counting. The record for the first is shared by Liverpool's Robbie Fowler and Everton's David Unsworth, after 82 minutes in 1997.

TRIVIA

Since 2009–10, only one England-born player has won Liverpool's Player of the Season, as voted for by fans. Who was it?

a) Jordan Henderson

b) Trent Alexander-Arnold

c) Jamie Carragher

”

It was a tough moment for me when I was in Senegal. I was born in a village and they don’t like football.

SADIO MANÉ

DID YOU KNOW...

The Liverpool women's team was established in 1989, becoming affiliated with the men's in 1994. They won the league in 2013 and 2014 having finished bottom in 2011 and 2012! The star in 2013 was Natasha Dowie, PFA Player of the Year with 13 goals in 14 games.

TRIVIA

When Liverpool won the 2019 FIFA Club World Cup final 1-0 against Brazilian side Flamengo, who scored the only goal, in the ninety-ninth minute?

a) Mo Salah

b) Adam Lallana

c) Roberto Firmino

”

At a club like Liverpool you always feel a bit of pressure. You should. But it doesn’t bother me.

VIRGIL VAN DIJK

DID YOU KNOW...

The first match ever broadcast in colour was Liverpool versus West Ham on 15 November 1969. Liverpool won 2–0, with goals to Chris Lawler and Bobby Graham. Graham was a right-back who played 549 games, quietly putting away an amazing 61 goals, earning the nickname "The Silent Knight".

TRIVIA

In 1998, Gérard Houllier became Liverpool's first foreign-born manager, but he shared the role with who?

a) Graeme Souness

b) Kenny Dalglish

c) Roy Evans

”

I even used to play as Liverpool on the PlayStation on FIFA when I was 18 or 19.

MO SALAH

DID YOU KNOW...

The most consecutive appearances for Liverpool is 417, by Phil Neal, between 1976 and 1983. In the latter year he suffered an injury against Manchester United that forced him to miss the following week's match against Sunderland. Roy Clemence is second with 336, followed by Bruce Grobbelaar on 317.

TRIVIA

Liverpool was the first English club to have a sponsor's logo on its shirt, in 1979. What brand was it?

a) Crown Paints

b) Hitachi

c) Dewhurst

”

I am a big soccer fan, and a very big Liverpool fan.

CLIVE OWEN

DID YOU KNOW...

Steven Gerrard has scored the most penalties in Liverpool history, with 47 of his 186 career goals coming from the spot. He scored a remarkable 82.5 per cent of penalties taken. But Jan Mølby was even better: with 42 out of 45 he scored 93.3 per cent! He scored 18 in a row – twice.

TRIVIA

Which Premier League manager's "first steady girlfriend", Doreen Carling, is the maternal grandmother of Liverpool star Trent Alexander-Arnold?

a) Roy Hodgson

b) Sam Allardyce

c) Alex Ferguson

”

Every time I put on a Liverpool shirt, I know it is more than just a football game.

FERNANDO TORRES

DID YOU KNOW...

In 1946, Jack Balmer became the only player to score three consecutive league hat-tricks for Liverpool, against Portsmouth, Derby County – four goals in fact – and Arsenal. In his 309 games for Liverpool, he scored 110 goals, and was part of the 1947 title-winning team.

?

TRIVIA

Which Japanese Liverpool player is in the Guiness Book of Records for performing 187 high-fives in one minute?

a) Wataru Endō

b) Takumi Minamino

c) Fūka Nagano

”

Liverpool without European football is like a banquet without wine.

ROY EVANS

DID YOU KNOW...

Steve Gerrard's ninety-first-minute equalizer against West Ham in the 2006 FA Cup Final is one of the greatest moments in Liverpool history. Struck from 35 yards from goal, it made the score 3–3, and Liverpool won the match on penalties, their first Cup win since 2000–01.

TRIVIA

Which famous English band featured Liverpool fans singing "You'll Never Walk Alone" on a 1971 album?

a) Pink Floyd

b) The Moody Blues

c) Deep Purple

”

Some people think football is a matter of life and death. I assure you, it's much more serious than that.

BILL SHANKLY

DID YOU KNOW...

He became known as the Supersub. David Fairclough scored 55 goals for Liverpool, with 18 coming in 62 outings as a substitute. It was his goal to win against Saint-Étienne in the 1977 European Cup in 1977 that made him a legend – Liverpool went on to win the tournament!

FINAL WORD

They are the greatest team of all, with more trophies than any other team in England, and more European titles. With some of the biggest names as players and managers, the Reds will always take top spot, and leave their rivals far behind in the battle for glory!

ANSWERS

8 b
11 b
14 b
17 a
20 a
23 c
26 b
29 c
32 c
35 c
38 a
41 b
44 b
47 c
50 c
53 c
56 b
59 b
62 a

65 a
68 c
71 b
74 c
77 b
80 b
83 a
86 c
89 c
92 c
95 b
98 a
101 c
104 c
107 b
110 c
113 b
116 a

Have you enjoyed this book? If so, find us on Facebook at **Summersdale Publishers**, on Twitter/X at **@Summersdale** and on Instagram and TikTok at **@summersdalebooks** and get in touch. We'd love to hear from you!

www.summersdale.com

Image credits

Male footballers © ednal/Shutterstock.com
Female footballers © Eli_Oz/Shutterstock.com
Shirt image © tomambroz/Shutterstock.com

Printed in Great Britain
by Amazon

63362149R00069